THE LAST VETERANS

of World War II

PORTRAITS AND MEMORIES

4880 Lower Valley Road • Atglen, PA 19310

RICHARD BELL

THE LAST VETERANS

of World War II

Foreword by Tim Weiner
Winner of the Pulitzer Prize and National Book Award

Other Schiffer Books on Related Subjects
Grunts: The Last US Draft, 1972 by Ed Eckstein (978-0-7643-5302-4)
World War II Posters by David Pollack (978-0-7643-5246-1)
The Doolittle Raid by Carroll V. Glines (978-0-88740-347-7)

Cover and book design by John P. Cheek
Type set in Adobe Garamond Pro

ISBN: 978-0-7643-5362-8
Printed in China

Published by Schiffer Publishing, Ltd.
4880 Lower Valley Road
Atglen, PA 19310
Phone: (610) 593-1777; Fax: (610) 593-2002
E-mail: Info@schifferbooks.com
www.schifferbooks.com

For our complete selection of fine books on this and related subjects, please visit our website at www.schifferbooks.com. You may also write for a free catalog.

Schiffer Publishing's titles are available at special discounts for bulk purchases for sales promotions or premiums. Special editions, including personalized covers, corporate imprints, and excerpts can be created in large quantities for special needs. For more information, contact the publisher.

We are always looking for people to write books on new and related subjects. If you have an idea for a book, please contact us at proposals@schifferbooks.com.

Contents

Foreword

"I hate war as only a soldier who has lived it can, only as one who has seen its brutality, its futility, its stupidity," Dwight D. Eisenhower said in 1946, a few months after the end of World War II. This was the general who led the D-Day invasion, and secured victory for America and its allies in Europe.

"We know something of the cost of that war," he said a decade later. "We were in it from December 7, 1941, until August of 1945. Ever since that time, we have been waging peace." This was a president midway through eight years in office—an era when few soldiers were sent overseas to die of shot and shell—a man determined to keep his powder dry and his citizenry safe. He knew what the costs of the next war could be. Would that each of his successors understood what it takes to wage peace.

We look at Richard Bell's photographs and we see America as it was—a human community united by a common humanity, the shared experience of having fought for freedom—and we see the America of our shared ideals. We are looking at the past in the hopes of seeing a better future. It's here in these images. Here is a woman who served as an Army nurse and healed wounded soldiers; you look at her and sense the horrors she has endured and the courage she summoned up to do her duty. There's a Navajo code talker whose untranslatable native tongue confounded the enemy; he looks proud of the essential role he and his tribesman played in securing victory in the Pacific. We might not know these people existed without Bell's images. Now they are immortalized in these pages.

Here is a hero you've heard of—John Paul Stevens, the intelligence officer turned Supreme Court Justice; he strived to preserve the liberties for which he and his fellow officers fought. Here's Harrison Dillard, a man who was famous long ago—in one photo he's the black infantryman in a still-segregated army, dreaming of the Olympics he would win, and in the other he's beaming with pride more than half a century later. He won four gold medals in 1948 and 1952.

And there is Hiroshi Miyamura, a native New Mexican, who won a far rarer medal. He served in a unique all-Nisei Army regiment during the war, when so many Japanese-Americans were uprooted from their homes and forcibly interned by the government of the United States. His story still astonishes. He was awarded the Medal of Honor for unimaginable acts of bravery during the Korean War—and the citation was classified "Top Secret," something unprecedented in American military history. Miyamura was captured and held as a prisoner of war for two years; if the enemy had known how many he had killed single-handedly (more than fifty) and how many of his fellow soldiers he had saved, he almost surely would have been tortured and killed. The war ended, the secrecy was lifted, the medal unsealed. President Eisenhower formally decorated Sgt. Miyamura at a White House ceremony on October 27, 1953; the citation speaks of his "indomitable heroism."

Miyamura went on to work as an auto mechanic and gas station owner, sent his three children to college, retired in his hometown of Gallup, and went fishing. At this writing he is ninety-one years old. I like to imagine him looking out over a running river, watching the light play on the water, his mind free of the brutality of war.

It was so long ago that it was a black-and-white world, in several senses. The images of the war were on black and white film. They came to us in black and white newspapers and newsreels. The armed forces of the United States were segregated; black troops were relegated to roles like cooking meals and digging graves.

The world itself was divided into good and evil. During the war, we made alliances with communists to fight fascists (and after the war, it was often the other way around). But Americans believed we were forces of light against forces of darkness. And we were, and we won. We became the most powerful force on earth, and that victory enabled us to move closer to becoming a democracy with liberty and justice for all. It seemed we were united then.

We are divided in so many ways today, our red states and our blue states, and yet so much unites us. The men and women you behold in this book represent the ideals of the United States. When our survival as a free republic was at stake, they fought shoulder to shoulder, in bunkers and trenches, in code rooms and sick bays, on land and sea, and they protected us from evil.

The people whose faces and hands you behold in these pages are among the last living souls who can summon up memories of the global battle against the Axis. We can honor them by remembering them. And they will live forever on these pages, after the last veteran of this war is laid to rest.

Tim Weiner
New York, February 2017

Tim Weiner is a former *New York Times* reporter, author of five books, and winner of the Pulitzer Prize and National Book Award. His most recent book is *One Man Against the World: The Tragedy of Richard Nixon.*

Preface

As a young boy in the 1950s I loved to look at *Life Magazine,* and *The Saturday Evening Post*. A vivid memory was seeing photos of Civil War veterans marching in a Veterans Day parade. I was awestruck seeing men connected to an event that felt as remote as ancient Rome to an eight-year-old boy. That is the seed that grew into this book.

My approach to presenting this feeling of awe is to create a visual moment where the past and present are linked. The enormity of time and diversity of experience are crystalized. The intent is to explore diversity in the World War II effort including service arm, gender, and ethnic origins. The black and white presentation mirrors the time. The penetrating gaze of the subjects recreates the ethos of the endeavor of war.

I'm in the generation destined to honor and pay forward the achievements of our fathers, the veterans of World War II. In that vein, the intent of this book is to enlighten and remind future generations about these courageous men and women as they tell their tales of understandable fear, grace, and sometimes, humor. Let us remember and honor them.

Acknowledgments

The most rewarding part of making this book was meeting and interviewing the veterans of World War II. I thank them for sharing their stories. And more than anything else, I thank them for their service.

The most difficult part was finding them. One would think that a government agency or a military agency would keep track of its veterans. They don't. Some veteran organizations do keep lists but cannot legally release any names or information, and thus the vets live in relative anonymity.

I managed to find these men and women in two ways: with the help of journalists around the country who work tirelessly reporting important events in the local press and by word of mouth. When I was looking for a Navajo code talker, for instance, a Google search turned up a story in a Phoenix newspaper by Brian Skoloff. A couple of phone calls later, Brian had helped me contact Roy Hawthorne, Navajo Code Talker. Thanks to Melanie Burney at *The Philadelphia Inquirer*. She helped put me in touch with someone from the battleship USS *New Jersey*. Thanks to Ruthie Millar at Clemson Downs in South Carolina. She welcomed me into their retirement community, home of many veterans. Ken Scar of Clemson University was also a great help. Thanks to everyone at Medford Leas in New Jersey, another beautiful retirement home with many veterans. And most of all, thanks to the families of the veterans.

I'm a photographer by trade, meaning I need a lot of help with my writing. Thanks to Suzanne Murphy and Tina Kaupe who gave me constant help as I struggled to put my sentences together. Thank you for the suggestions and proofreading.

Mike Molle, 92
MARINES
1st Division

PELELIU, OKINAWA

"I loved being a Marine. I was young and looking for adventure. I got it.

"First came Peleliu. That was really nasty. I spent my first night in battle sleeping in an LST (Landing Ship, Tank) boat. At 0400, the boat let us out 300 yards from shore. We were sitting ducks. Bullets were hitting all around us. Our commander, Chesty Puller, only knew one command: 'Go Straight Ahead!' They almost drove us off the beach.

"On Okinawa, we chased the Japanese in the mountains. There were no frontlines. I dropped my mortar baseplate on my hand and broke it. I was told to go to the rear for treatment and they wanted to send me to a hospital ship. I said 'no way.' I wanted to rejoin my men, so I went off by myself. I knew the general direction but I was in no-man's-land. It was the stupidest thing I ever did, running around for four hours. I could have been found by a Japanese platoon and that would have been it. I heard voices and miraculously it was my crew. In the morning, my lieutenant saw me and said, 'What are you doing here, you can't even pick up a gun with that hand!' I was sent to Saipan to recover but I got dengue fever, jungle rot, and malaria there in the hospital."

John Lauriello, 92
MARINES
5th Division

IWO JIMA

John was in the first assault wave at Red Beach, Iwo Jima. He remembers the battle this way.

"We left Hawaii, New Year's Day 1945. We didn't know where we were going. For fifty days we zig-zagged at twelve knots. They treated us like mushrooms, kept us in the dark, and fed us horse shit. Finally, we arrive at our destination and [are] told to prepare for battle and assemble on deck. We load into the landing craft and wait and circle while all the boats are filled. We're bobbing on the ocean, the smells are overwhelming. Diesel fumes, throw-up, and guys shitting their pants. We start for the beach, but first we have to go through a dense smoke screen the Navy has put down for our benefit. We suddenly come out the other side and there it is, a big barren gray rock in the middle of the ocean. All hell breaks loose.

"The gate goes down, I pull my radio cart off the boat and it sinks. Machine gun fire raining down like water from a shower head. My friend Paul, a Navajo code talker, gets killed immediately. I dig in for the night. Thirty-eight days pass, all the same intensity. On one of the last days, about 300 Nips come out of nowhere with swords and spears. We're in the showers. The butcher, the bakers and the candlestick makers, who are all Marine riflemen, pick up their guns and mow them down. The battle for Iwo Jima is over."

Harlan Twible, 94
NAVY

USS *INDIANAPOLIS*

Harlan graduated from the the US Naval Academy in 1945. His first duty was as ensign aboard the new cruiser USS *Indianapolis*. The ship was to deliver the atomic bomb components to a small island in the South Pacific, called Tinian. It was a secret mission and no one was told what the containers held.

"When they brought it aboard it looked like a capsule they used for x-ray in the hospital. I thought it was radium and it was needed out in the Pacific for x-ray use. They brought a great big box thing and welded it to the deck. The capsule was put in a stateroom. Everybody's attention was on the box welded to the deck. We didn't know what it was, nobody knew. No one had ever heard of the atomic bomb. We weren't told what it was, we had no idea. We delivered it to Tinian.

"We left Tinian to join the fleet after a couple of days. We left without an escort so no one knew where we were. We were hit at midnight with two torpedoes. The bow was blown off. I was told by my executive officer to get the men to the high side, but it was impossible. I gave the order to abandon ship. Nobody did. So I said, 'Follow me!' and 325 men followed me into the water. I read an article recently about me and it said I had saved 151 men. I didn't save them, they saved themselves. We were in the water four days, five nights. A lot of guys died of hypothermia. We kept ourselves tied together in a net. We kept the sharks away as long as we stayed together in the group."

They were found by a patrol plane on a routine mission. The navy did not know they had sunk.

John Paul Stevens, 96
NAVY
Communications and Intelligence

US SUPREME COURT JUSTICE

"When I actually went on duty, I was not deciphering messages, [but] I ended up doing traffic analysis—at Pearl Harbor, Hawaii—which is regarding the external characteristics of messages and trying to get intelligence without reading them. I would look at the call signs and frequencies and the people who were sending and receiving them. You can derive an amazing amount of intelligence without knowing what the message actually says."

When asked about personal anecdotes from the war, Justice Stevens briefly mentions one off-hours activity.

"I fondly remember going out to Makapuu Beach for body surfing. It's wonderful, best surf in the world on that particular beach. A couple of young officers and I went out there periodically."

Getting back to business quickly, Stevens went on.

"But the most important military accomplishment I participated in was … the Japanese started encoding their call signs. I worked with a young yeoman named Stanley Moe, a brilliant guy who specialized in studying the traffic [messages] originating at weather stations. You could decipher them pretty easily because they had standard form … like wind direction, wind speed, stuff like that. So when the Japanese began to encode their call signs, which was a new

development, he and I worked together figuring out what their new code was. We succeeded in figuring it out in maybe 48–72 hours. We worked straight through until we figured the thing out … and that experience stands out very graphically in my mind.

"I was on duty when the confirmation of the Adm. Yamamoto shoot down came in. So I was a witness but not a participant in that operation. I have expressed some mixed feelings about that operation. It's very unusual to have an individual as a target of a military operation. But then actually the same thing happened with Osama Bin Laden. There was a difference because Osama Bin Laden was a bad guy and Adm. Yamamoto was a distinguished officer, a very highly regarded professional."

On a historical note, Justice Stevens is a huge Chicago Cubs baseball fan and had just returned from a 2016 World Series game when we spoke. I congratulated him, and he said, "You know, I was at the last Cubs World Series, in 1932. I was there and saw Babe Ruth's called shot. He pointed to the center field bleachers with his bat and hit the next pitch for a home run."

"You know when the guns stop and all that is over, that's when those fellas' real battle began."

Genevieve Smith, Army Nurse

See page 23

Genevieve Smith, 95
ARMY
Nurse Corps

103rd STATION HOSPITAL

"I met another girl who went in [the Army] at the same time. She and I stayed together for the whole war. We were so anxious to go someplace, but not stay here. Outside the dining room at Fort Dix, New Jersey, there was a big bulletin board. It had many notices for needing a cadre of nurses to go to so-and-so place. Peggy and I signed them all, until eventually they put up a sign: 'Lt. Murray and Lt. Smith, Please do not sign everything!'"

Lt. Smith ended up going to North Africa, Italy, and France. She was with the 103rd Station Hospital. It was made up of fifty nurses, thirty-five doctors, and enlisted men. She explained there were three levels of care. The first, closest to the front, was a triage center. Next was the station hospital where the immediate surgeries were done. Further away was the general hospital for surgeries that could wait and rehabilitation.

"It wasn't fun what we did, but it was exciting at that age. The thing I think most about are those patients we had. You know when the guns stop and all of that is over, that's when those fellas' real battle began. For some of them it was a battle for life, others got better and did all right. But for some, it never ended.

"I was in for four years. I left the Army at the end of the war. I'd had it! It took me a long time to get my uniform off. I had gone into New York and bought all new civilian clothes. Every time I'd put them on, I thought, that's a funny looking thing, and go back to my uniform. Then one day, I said to myself, this is getting funny now. You better take it off and leave it off."

Jerry Yellin, 92
ARMY AIR FORCE
P-51 Pilot, 78th Fighter Squadron

IWO JIMA

Jerry was the product of the Depression era. He sold magazine subscriptions door-to-door when he was a kid. As part of his pay he got coupons for prizes. He always used them to get balsa wood airplanes.

"At a briefing, we were shown a relief map of an island called Iwo Jima. As we banked into the Iwo Jima airfield, I looked out of my cockpit and I saw mounds and mounds and mounds of Japanese bodies being pushed into mass graves. The smells, the sights, the sounds were just overwhelming. The smell of 28,000 rotting bodies never leaves you. We strafed everything for thirty days.

"I made nineteen total missions over Japan escorting B-29s and strafing military targets. I was over Tokyo when the first atomic bomb was dropped. That was August 6th. My last mission was August 14, 1945. We had dropped the second bomb on Nagasaki and the Japanese hadn't surrendered. My wing man, Lt. Phillip Schlamberg, said to me, 'If we go, I'm not coming back, it's just a feeling.' I said just stay close to me and you'll be OK. On the return flight from Tokyo, I looked over at Phil and gave him the thumbs up. He returned the thumbs up. We banked into some clouds. When we came out, Phil was gone. Nobody saw or heard anything. We got back to Iwo and found out the war had been over for three hours. So Phil Schlamberg was the last man killed in combat in World War II.

"In 1988, my son married the daughter of a Japanese pilot which took me from hatred to love of family. I have three Japanese grandchildren. I'd like their contemporaries to know that my grandchildren's grandparents served their (respective) countries with honor. That war was an atrocity, but evil has to be wiped out. We are all the same in the eyes of nature. We are all human beings … exactly the same."

Joe Kite, 92
MARINES
6th Division

OKINAWA • CHINA • BRAZIL

Joe was in the first group of Marines to leave the states on December 14, 1941, with an assignment in Brazil. Mission: to ask the Germans and Italians to leave an airfield in Recife, Brazil. After sizing up the situation, they left, and the field became a staging area for resupplying the Pacific war.

He spent eighteen months in Brazil, and then went on to Okinawa, one of the hardest fought battles of the war. Joe can't bring himself to speak in any specifics about what he did there. It was the largest amphibious assault of the war and it became the staging area for the final assault on Japan. Joe remembers hearing the bomb had been dropped and war was over. But there was more to come.

Joe went to China in the occupying force and because he had some prior experience, was made fire chief of the Suzhou, China, fire department. This gives him the most pride of his war experiences. The Chinese infrastructure was in shambles because of the civil war going on between the Communists and Nationalists. The Marine fire brigade acted as the local fire department.

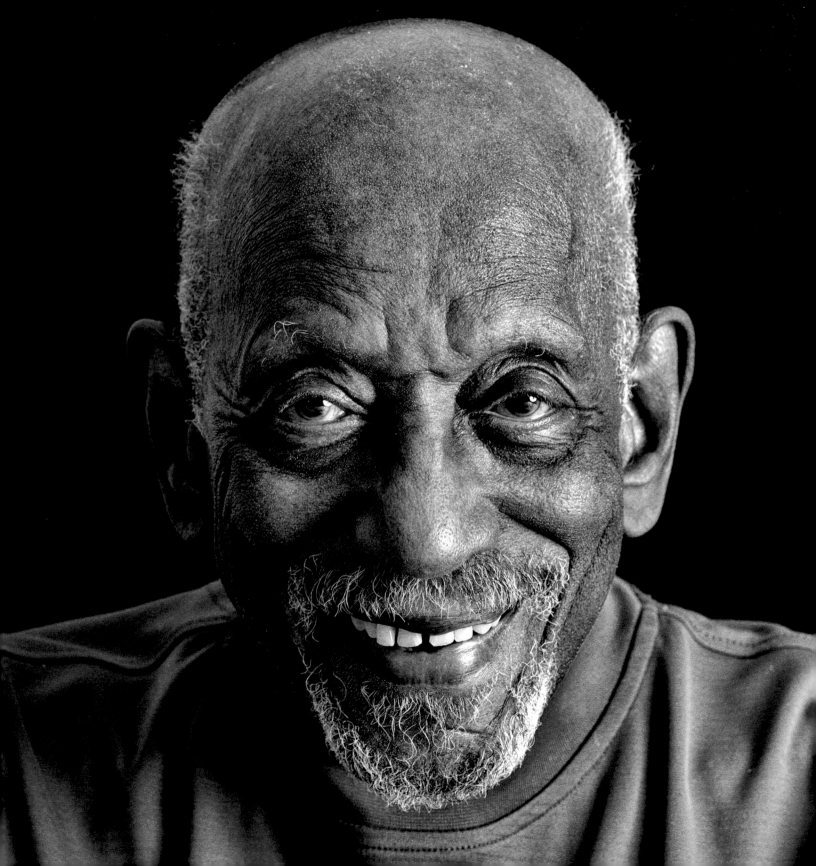

Harrison Dillard, 93
ARMY
92nd Infantry

ITALY

Harrison Dillard spent seventeen months in Italy including seven months of combat. After the war ended, the 92nd Infantry became the Army of Occupation and started to relax. A track meet was proposed between the European and the Mediterranean Campaign troops. Mr. Dillard won several races.

"It was in Frankfurt and Gen. Patton was in attendance. I was standing there with him when he was asked by reporters what he thought about this athlete from the Mediterranean Campaign, and Gen. Patton says 'That's the best goddamn athlete I've ever seen.' I thought that was quite a compliment.

"We guarded the German POWs during the occupation. We didn't make any friends. I remember once, one incident. Of course as African-Americans, and the times, and if you're in the states there's still Jim Crow and all of that still existed anyway. I can remember one time the Germans were assigned to KP and were dishing out the food and this one guy from our outfit (all-black 92nd Infantry), he got upset because the prisoner was giving him lip about how much food he was supposed to give him, and boy, he took out and he went over the counter after this guy. Non-commissioned officers had to separate them. So we did not make any friends."

Olympics, Four Gold Medals

After leaving the army, Mr. Dillard went on to become one of the greatest Olympic athletes of all time. He was the only man to win gold medals in both the 100 meter dash and 110 meter hurdles in an Olympic career (1948 and 1952).

Maurice Berry, 92
ARMY
104th Infantry Regiment

BATTLE OF THE BULGE

"We landed in continental Europe ninety-three days after D-Day. By the time we joined Gen. Patton's 3rd Army, the Battle of the Bulge was starting. We were just in time to be the lead regiment in the counterattack at the Bulge. We walked sixteen miles through sleet, snow, rain, and very cold temperatures to reach the point of combat. I was wounded by two grenades and spent thirty-five days in the hospital. While I was there, Gen. Patton came through and actually stopped at my bed. I must have had some nerve, but I asked him 'How are the casualties?' and he said, 'Not bad.' I knew he was lying. When I got back to my company there had been one-hundred percent turnover.

"During the occupation I was stationed in Linz, Austria as an MP. One day two guys drag in a half-dressed, loopy-in-the-head prison camp guard from Mauthausen Concentration Camp. We call headquarters and turn him over for processing. One of the guys stays behind and he turns out to have been interned at that concentration camp. His name is Murray. He befriends me and we become lifelong best friends. He's a Polish Jew and he recognizes me as Jewish also. One night there in Austria we are playing poker and Murray is sleeping. He suddenly starts screaming, 'They killed my mother, they killed my sister, they killed my father.' He was having a nightmare. We let him get it out of his system. He never again spoke to me about his family again."

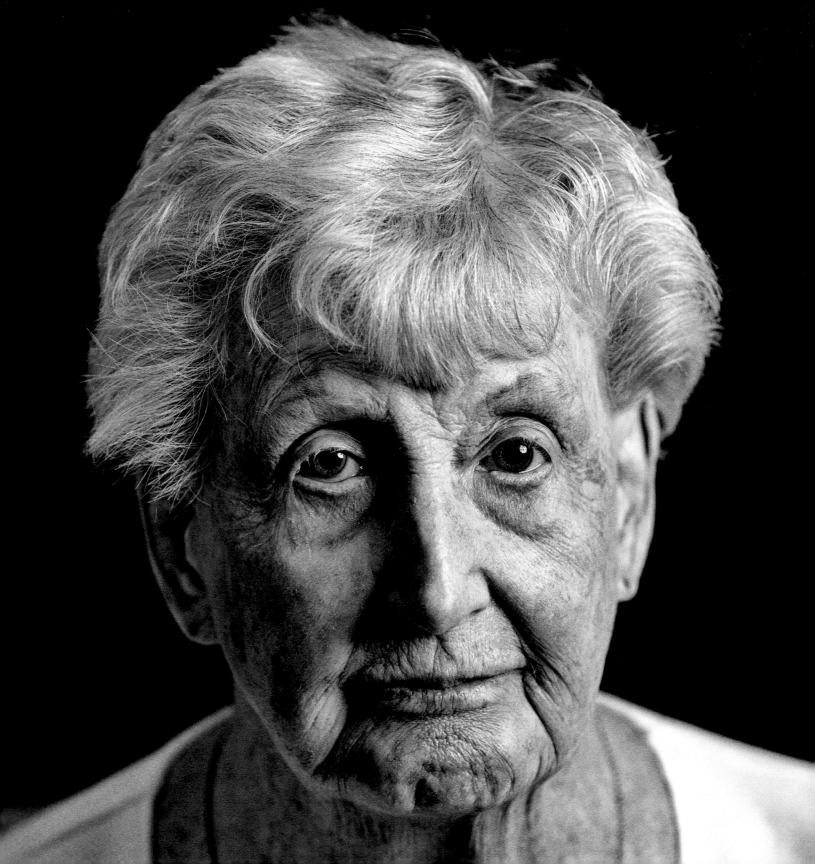

Charlotte Bart, 93
COAST GUARD

CHARLESTON, SOUTH CAROLINA

Charlotte joined the Coast Guard in 1944, and was stationed in Charleston, South Carolina. "It was a wonderful experience," she said with great pride. She has remained active to this day with Coast Guard and Marine associations and programs.

She worked as a transportation specialist, trained to operate the "Duck" boat which went on land and sea, as well as jeeps, trucks, and four-wheel drive vehicles. Charleston had a variety of severe weather including hurricanes, which made for challenging circumstances for transportation. Charlotte remembers having to pick up some officers from their homes by boat because of hurricane flooding.

The "Duck" boat is still in use today as a tourist vehicle in many cities, including Philadelphia.

Herbert Stevens, 95
ARMY
Artillery Mechanic

EUROPEAN CAMPAIGN

The use of artillery reached its zenith in World War II. The technical development between the world wars, particularly in the United States, created a system that was second to none. In many postwar interviews, German soldiers mentioned the fear that American artillery created along the frontlines.

Stevens, ninety-five, served as an army artillery mechanic in World War II. He met his wife, a native Parisian, in a dance hall during the spontaneous celebrations that followed the Liberation of Paris in 1944.

Herbert says his proudest memory of the war is the bombing of Nuremberg Stadium. "They had swastikas hung up like Yankee championship banners. We shelled it until it was dust."

Hiroshi "Hershey" Miyamura, 91
ARMY
442nd All Nisei Regiment

ITALY, OCCUPATION
KOREA, 7th REGIMENT
MEDAL OF HONOR RECIPIENT

Hershey was drafted in January 1945. He joined the 442nd Regiment and five days from landing in Naples, Italy, the war ended. He spent a year there in the Army of Occupation processing German prisoners.

In the Korean War, Hershey was awarded the Medal of Honor. Here are his words:

"On April 24, 1951, my squad, a heavy weapons machine gun unit were suddenly threatened by an overwhelming force. Instead of losing all my men, I told them to withdraw and I would cover their withdrawal. I had a machine gun, a rifle with bayonet, [and] that's what I did a lot of my damage with. The machine gun jammed and I destroyed it. I had to use hand-to-hand combat. I don't know how I survived that. I wasn't thinking, I was just doing what I had to do to survive." He is credited with killing at least sixty enemy soldiers, many without the aid of weapons.

"My squad all made it back. I was captured and spent twenty-seven months in a North Korean prison camp. After, I put the war out of my mind. That's how I was able to survive all these years. I wanted to start a family and run a business." He acknowledged that he had made it possible for a bunch of other guys to do the same. "I feel good about that."

President Eisenhower awarded the Medal of Honor to Hershey in 1953. At the ceremony, Hershey remembers the president coming over to him before it began. "I'm standing there waiting for the ceremony to start and the president comes over and says, 'Son, I see you are a little nervous.' I say, 'Yes sir, I've never done this before.' He leans in closer and says, 'Me, too. I've never done this before either.' That made me feel so much better."

Harry Garbe, 93
MARINES
5th Amphibious Corps

IWO JIMA

Harry told me he was a lousy shot in basic training. His friends became riflemen and that's what he wanted, but it was not to be. He was assigned to duties that he described as being, "in the rear, with the gear."

It's known that for every soldier pulling the trigger on the frontline, there are at least three soldiers in the rear making it possible.

"We're loading a truck with white crosses and the sarge says, 'Take them up to the cemetery.' We drove up to the cemetery where we see marines being buried. They're digging long trenches and laying about fifty marines side by side, each three feet apart in the trench. The dog tags were placed in their mouths so when they are recovered they'll know who they are and where they should be sent in the states. A soldier comes up with a small camera and starts taking pictures of this. Someone complained, I guess, because the sergeant comes up and says, 'What are you doing?' and the guy says, 'I want to remember this.' The sergeant picks this guy up, throws him in the trench and says, 'If want to remember this, start helping bury these guys.'

"After Iwo, my group went back to Hawaii to train for the invasion of Japan. They gave us a long talk about what to expect. I'll never forget what they said, 'Take a look around, the man to your right will be wounded and the man to your left will be killed.' I looked around and saw

every man in the hall looking to see if they were the man in the middle.

"The day came when we were to leave for the Japanese invasion. My group was split in two, with one group leaving at 10:00 pm and my group leaving in the morning. My group was told to pack up the tents and gear and be ready in the morning. The sergeant comes up to us in the morning and says, 'OK now, put the tents back up!' We all think, yea, just like the military, and collectively groan. Sarge says, 'What should you care, the Japanese surrendered, the war is over.' I was lucky again, the first group that already left went all the way to Japan and became the Army of Occupation. And I went home."

"We didn't know about the code talkers when we signed up. It was a secret … We broke the Japanese secret code but they never broke ours."

Roy Hawthorne, Marines, Navajo Code Talker

See page 45

Dr. John Rudolph, 104
ARMY MEDICAL SERVICE GROUP
61st Station Hospital

NORTH AFRICAN CAMPAIGN • ITALIAN CAMPAIGN

Dr. Rudolph was a thirty-year-old doctor with a successful practice when he joined the Army Medical Service. He put his practice on hold and spent three years in Africa and Italy as a frontline doctor.

The 61st Station Hospital was formed intact from Cooper Hospital in Camden, New Jersey. They were the first civilian hospital group to be accepted by the War Department in World War II as a station hospital.

Over the next three years, the 61st treated more than 20,000 men wounded in combat in North Africa, Sicily, and Italy. After moving to Italy, the 61st came under fire on occasion, but didn't suffer any casualties as a result.

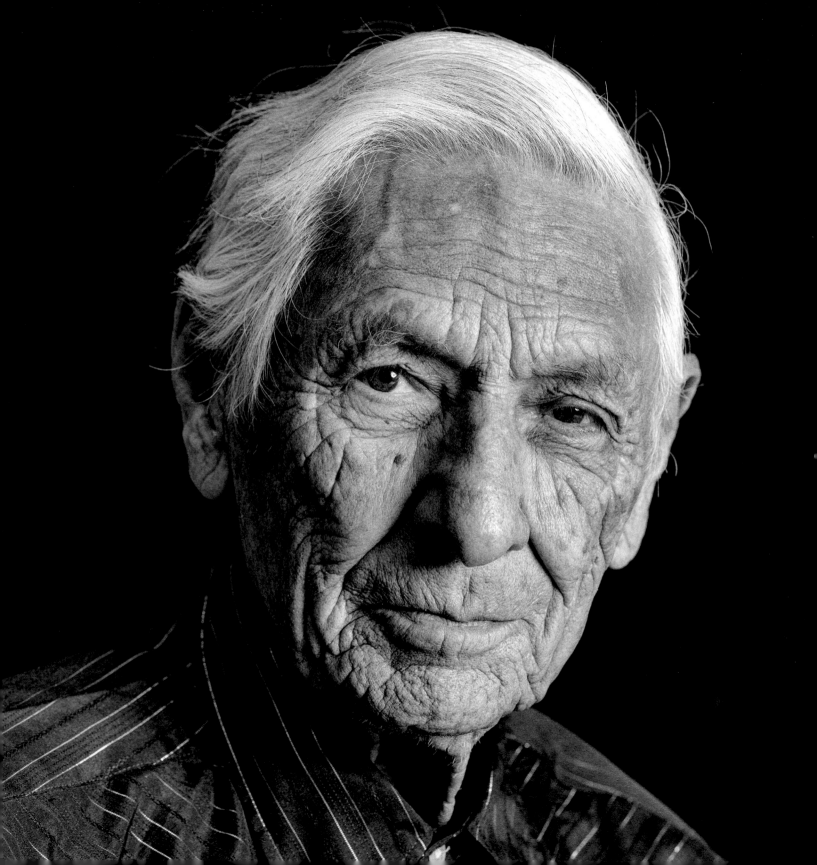

Roy Hawthorne, 91
MARINES
Navajo Code Talker

GUADALCANAL • OKINAWA

Roy was one of the Navajo code talkers, who served to make our military messages indecipherable to the Japanese in the Pacific War. He was born and raised in the Navajo Nation located in the "four corners" of the American southwest. It is the largest sovereign nation inside another sovereign nation in the world. Roy is still there today driving his pickup truck and being a great ambassador for his god, his people, and the American way.

"We didn't know about the code talkers when we signed up. It was a secret. The recruiter just said they wanted Navajos for special assignments. The secret of the Navajo code talkers was a secret as secure as the atomic bomb Manhattan Project. We broke the Japanese secret code but they never broke ours."

Once while pinned down under heavy fire on Okinawa, Roy made a call for an airstrike using the code and only knowing it went through when the planes arrived. Years later while reminiscing with a fellow code talker about this incident the other code talker said, "That was me getting your message, I remember. I was on a battleship at sea." The code talkers kept their secret for over twenty years after the war, not even telling family what they did in the war. When the government lifted the secrecy and they could finally talk about what they did, Roy dryly said, "I'm glad they gave us twenty-three years to make up some good war stories."

Anne Hargreaves, 93
ARMY
Nurse

135th EVACUATION HOSPITAL

"I was in Gen. Patton's Army. He was awful to the boys, terrible. He would come on the wards and say, 'What's he doin' here?' and you'd end up saying, 'He's a battle casualty' [now known as Post Traumatic Stress Disorder]. And then he would go after the boys. He'd say, 'What are you doin' here, get back in there and help your colleagues.' I couldn't stand it. It was so distressing to me because we couldn't do anything for them. That's why, when I got back in this country, I went into psychiatry for the rest of my professional life.

"In 1943, I signed up. Had one month of army training. Let me tell you what happened to me after that. I got in the boat … you go in a convoy on the way over … I was in a crash in the convoy. The front of our boat ran into another boat. We were told to abandon ship. They had taught us how to abandon ship, but I had skipped the class 'cause I thought I'd never be abandoning ship. I got up on deck and I'm terrified. I'm shakin', shakin', shakin'. They told us to push back, push back, to get the front of the ship out of the water. A doctor came over to me and held me and said, 'Everything's going to be all right.' And I thought to myself, 'Oh no! I skipped the abandon ship class, I never learned to swim, and I never screwed with my boyfriend before I left!' Those were my three greatest regrets.

"I hear the shootin.' I'm told when I leave my tent, 'Be careful because you can be picked off by snipers.' We are the closest hospital to the shootin.' We pick 'em up, give

them firsthand care to keep them from dying. Put them not in an ambulance, usually an airplane, to fly them back to a general hospital where they can do major surgery. We didn't do major stuff, we did emergency stuff. I saw the '*M*A*S*H*' TV show. I thought I was back in the field. It's just like that, but I don't remember the people being as crazy as they were in '*M*A*S*H.'"

Ted Drought, 93
NAVY
Submariner

USS *BERGALL*

"I went into the Navy with a buddy from high school. All along he wanted submarines and I wanted electrician's mate. I hated submarines—I always sleep with the windows open! When it came to passing out the assignments, he got electricians mate, and I got submarines. I guess it's bound to happen.

"On December 13, 1944, the *Bergall* engaged the Japanese cruiser *Myōkō*. Both ships were damaged. *Bergall* had to end her patrol after being hit by a dud eight-inch shell. *Myōkō* sailed to Singapore and was never repaired.

"I was on lookout, the ship we hit was on fire. Suddenly, a powerful light came on and we were hit with eight-inch shells. Our torpedo door was shot off. We couldn't submerge. The captain got us together and told us our orders were to scuttle the ship in Borneo and spend the rest of the war in the mountains with the natives. He said, 'What do you think about that?' We said we didn't like it. He said, 'We'll try for Australia then.' Our captain was called to task for disobeying orders but was exonerated. He did save the ship.

"We made it to Perth and the ship was repaired. While we waited, we were busy hunting for women. I met a gal of pretty good size. We liked to jitterbug and we cleared space when we did it." With a big laugh, Ted says, "I called her Miss Eight-foot Circle."

Ernest Kaufman, 96
BORN IN GERMANY
Inmate at Buchenwald Concentration Camp, Released 1938

JOINED US ARMY IN 1943

Ernest Kaufman was born in Germany. He was arrested along with his family during the infamous *Kristallnacht* and sent to Buchenwald Concentration Camp. He secured a release just before the war started and immigrated to the US in 1939. His family was lost in the Holocaust. Mr. Kaufman tells many stories. Here is one.

"We were waiting to attack outside a small town. A man comes out through the lines from the town of Einbeck, Saxony, and asked us for help to save his town. There was a German military garrison in the town and they were going to put up a fight. I, like a stupid idiot, put a white rag on my Jeep and drove into town. German soldiers stopped me. I was scared to death. I told them my commanding officer wanted to speak to their commanding general. I made that up. They wanted to know how I knew German so well. I told them I went to college. I was taken to the commanding general's office. I told the general, who didn't say a word, I had orders from my commanding officer that he must immediately surrender or we will attack, destroy the town, and he would be held responsible for all loss of life and property. The general didn't say a word. Had me taken out of the office. Fifteen minutes later I was called back in. The general says that in order to save the town and its people, he had decided to accompany me back to our headquarters and surrender. The next thing I know, shaking like a leaf, I'm riding in the front seat of a Mercedes staff car with two German generals in the back seat. Close behind, 300 German officers and enlisted men were marching with us. I took the generals to our command post. Of course, my commanding officer, Col.

Biddle, was surprised as hell when I walked in with two German generals. The generals were outraged that they had to surrender to someone of lower rank. I told them they had to do it. They put their pistols on the desk.

"If at any time they had put together that I was an escaped German Jew, and just five years before, had been sitting in a concentration camp, I would have been shot on the spot."

Ernest authored a book called *From Fright to Fight to Farm*, published in 2016.

"We had to eat at tables behind a curtain [going south on the train] so the white people couldn't see us. That was our introduction to segregation in the South."

George Hardy, Army Air Force, Tuskegee Airman, P-51 Fighter Pilot

See page 57

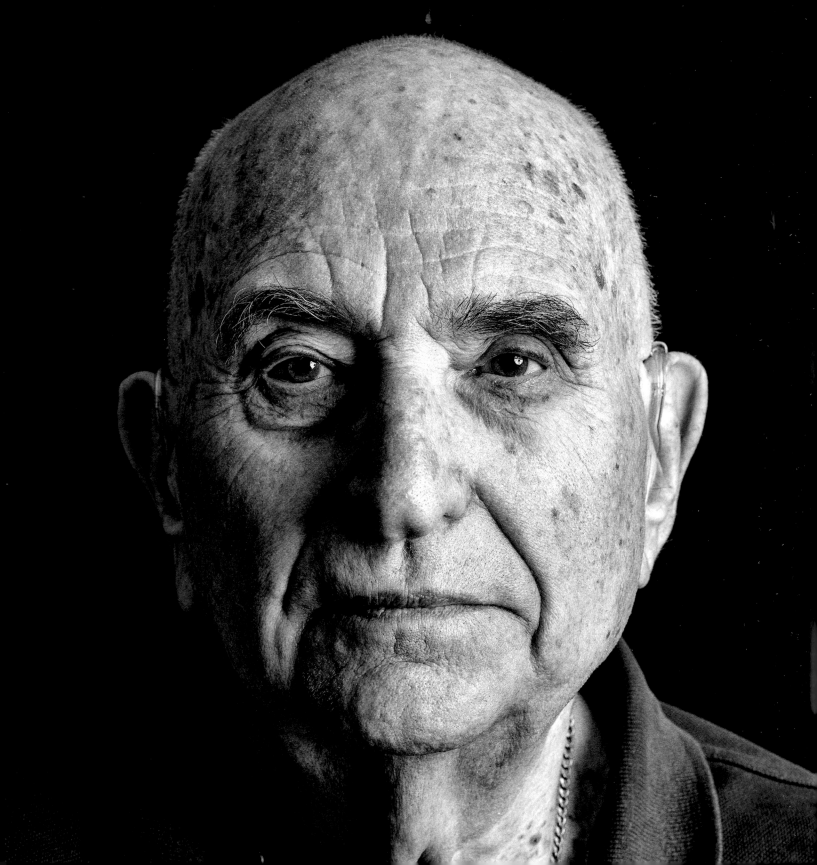

George Rubin, 92
ARMY AIR FORCE
18 Missions, B-17 Gunner

POW, GERMANY

"We were on a bombing mission to Munich. There was very intense flak and we were being decimated. One engine knocked out, one on fire. We tried to make Switzerland but couldn't. The pilot did a great job getting us down into a small opening in the mountains. We got out and were surrounded by teenagers in military uniforms, who immediately lined us up to be shot. A single officer from the regular army comes running up and stops the execution. Instead we were marched into the small town where the townspeople had lined up and they beat the shit out of us with brooms, shovels, and sticks while we were marched through the streets. It was called Sonthofen, Germany.

"We were taken to a series of prison camps, ending up in Moosburg, a camp with over 80,000 prisoners. On one of the marches between camps we were strafed by our own planes. We started making 'POW' signs on the autobahn with toilet paper when we heard the planes coming, and that worked.

"Our generation was told, 'We were heroes, now put the war away.' As the years went by, my nightmares got worse and worse. I took myself to the veterans administration and found out I had a very bad case of PTSD. I saw psychologists weekly. One time my doctor said, 'George, have you ever thought about going back to Germany as a sense of closure?' I wrote to the mayor of that town in Germany and got back a wonderful letter. He said not only do we want you to come, but we have memorabilia for you we saved hoping someday one of you would come back. We went back in 2000 and

visited all the places I had been. Everyone was great. It was very helpful and I got a sense of closure. I feel great."

George Hardy, 92
ARMY AIR FORCE
Tuskegee Airman, P-51 Fighter Pilot

21 COMBAT MISSIONS

Of the 355 Tuskegee airmen who went overseas and saw combat, about twenty still survive, according to Lt. Col. George Hardy, who is one of them.

Col. Hardy flew in World War II (P-51), Korea (B-29), and Vietnam (gunship). With twenty-eight years active service, he retired in 1971.

"When I grew up in Philadelphia we didn't have racial segregation, but there was racism. On our way to basic Army training in Mobile, Alabama, was where we saw segregation for the first time. We stopped in Cincinnati to change trains. That's where the south begins. Up until then we shared the dining car and Pullman car with whites. The change we noted was when we went to the dining car to eat. They had a big heavy curtain across the aisle. We had to eat at tables behind that curtain so the white people couldn't see us. That was our introduction to segregation in the South.

"The P-51 was fast, sleek and very maneuverable. It also had range. We could stay with the bombers all the way to Berlin and back. We were at Ramitelli Airbase in Italy. We picked up the bombers on their way to targets in Germany. We encountered a few Me 262s, the German jet fighter, a few times. We would turn toward them and they would fly away. They were faster than us. They didn't take us on at that point. They had been fighting since 1939 and were running out of planes and pilots. It had become a war of attrition. We could outproduce them and train our pilots in safety."

Bernie Vernick, 95
NAVY
Shipfitter 1st Class

LST 983, D-DAY LANDING AT "JUNO" BEACH

Bernie got drafted in 1942, but didn't want to be in the Army, so he enlisted in the Navy. With his experience of working at the Philadelphia Navy Yard he became a shipfitter. He was qualified in sheet metal, plumbing, and welding.

He spent his first eighteen months at Guantanamo Bay Navy Base in Cuba. From there he went to England and prepared for the D-Day landing. He was assigned to the LST 983, a landing ship that was as large as a football field. It carried thirty tanks, and all the men required to crew them. They landed on the first day at Juno Beach, the Canadian beachhead. The ship made fifty-two crossings of the English Channel until the war was over. Their cargo included replacement troops, equipment, and fuel. German prisoners would be on the returning part of the crossings.

Bernie says, "You know I'm Jewish. There were three of us on board—another shipfitter and the cook. The cook got ulcers of all things, so they sent him home. When the Germans were on board, we'd go look at them." With disdain he adds, "I couldn't stand them."

"I remember clearly our last trip. The war is over. We picked up a crew of British soldiers in Hamburg, Germany. We sailed up the Elbe River into the North Sea, then down a fjord into Oslo, Norway. It's beautiful. We get a night off and go into town to a restaurant. The beer looks pretty good, like American beer. We were sick of the warm English beer. We start to drink, the beer is flat, no alcohol. We ask want happened and they tell us the Germans had taken all the alcohol for fuel in the war."

Bernie likes to talk to his last surviving uncle almost every day, who is also a veteran. That's right, Bernie is part of five generations of living family!

Allyn Rickett, 95
MARINES
5th Division

IWO JIMA

Allyn Rickett was an interrogation officer. He had a working knowledge of Japanese and Chinese. He landed on Iwo Jima on the first day.

"We landed on Iwo the first day, but late in the day. I was with a group of signal corpsmen. We got to the shore about 6:00 pm under heavy Japanese mortar fire. I dived for what a thought was a foxhole and the Marines yelled, 'Get out of there, that's the latrine!'

"We got very few prisoners. When the Marines got tired of shooting into a cave they would call for the language interpreter to talk the Japanese out of the cave. That didn't work. [But] I had two prisoners that were Catholics and that's why they had surrendered. They were delightful characters and I relied on these two guys. For instance, I went out one time and took them with me. Six or seven Japanese soldiers came running out of a cave. All I had was a carbine. I took the gun and pulled back the bolt and it dropped out on the ground and that was the only time I attempted to fire a shot in the whole Iwo Jima campaign. One of the Japanese [Catholic] prisoners picked it up and handed it back to me.

"We went into Japan as the first wave of the occupying army. One time we went down to Nagasaki and we had no idea about radiation. We visited a hospital and the stench of decaying flesh, uhhh, you can smell it a mile away. I was left with a terrible dilemma because if it hadn't been for the atomic bomb, I would be dead. We were scheduled to land

Photo in hand: Allyn Rickett is seen on the right smoking a pipe. The other two men are not identified. Taken on Iwo Jima with Mt. Suribachi in the background, site of the Marine flag raising.

in Japan, first wave. But on the other hand, I saw the destruction the Japanese people endured. After landing they couldn't be more cooperative. They just accepted that the war was over."

Stanley Lawruk, 92
ARMY AIR FORCE
B-17 Flight Engineer

PEENEMÜNDE, GERMANY • FRANCE

Stanley was on his twenty-fourth mission over Germany. Their target, Peenemünde, was the German secret missile base, where the V-1 and V-2 rockets were built to be fired against targets in Great Britain. His B-17 came under heavy enemy fire and lost both engines on the right side. He and his crew had three choices: bailout over Germany and be captured, ditch in the Baltic Sea and swim, or try for Sweden, a neutral country.

They crashed landed in Sweden. Although they couldn't leave the country, the Germans demanded that enemy combatants be detained by the neutral country. After spending six months in what he calls "hotel living" conditions, they were exchanged for German prisoners.

Stanley also flew three missions over France for the D-Day invasion, bombing German installations along the coast and inland. "I shot at many German fighters and saw them go down, but I can't claim I did it, because a lot of us were shooting at the same planes."

Arthur Gendler, 93
ARMY
7th Armored Division

NORMANDY, OMAHA BEACH
D-DAY, DAY ONE

"It was around 6:30 am and we started loading the LST (landing craft). I was going in to Omaha Beach with the infantry. I was armored division but my bucket gun was going in at Utah Beach because of the water depths. My lieutenant told me I was going to use a rifle that shot grenades and rockets instead of my M1 rifle. 'Why me?' I asked. He says, 'Because you had the highest score with it at training camp.' 'Yea,' I say, 'but I was only shooting blanks.' There I was in the LST and the door drops down and the two guys on either side of me get picked off, they never step off the boat. I parked myself and kneeled down on the beach, put a rocket on the gun and fired at a muzzle flash of a canon in a bunker. I hit it. It blew up. That was one purpose I served that nobody knew about. Then I started firing grenades up there. Grenades are coming down and we're throwing them back up again. It was chaos on the beach. We got our bucket gun from Utah Beach. German fighters came in trying to get us off the beach and we had fun picking them off.

"Just before the [Battle of the Bulge] we ran over a mine. The whole truck and gun blew up. I was driving. I went flying. When the medics found me I was still holding the steering wheel. I was OK but my hearing was temporally gone. The next day we got another truck and gun and kept going."

Photo in hand: Arthur Gendler is on left. The other veteran is unidentified.

Mort Walker, 93
ARMY

ITALY
CREATOR OF *BEETLE BAILEY* COMICS

"I had an almost fabulous war experience. It was a whole learning experience. Four years of research.

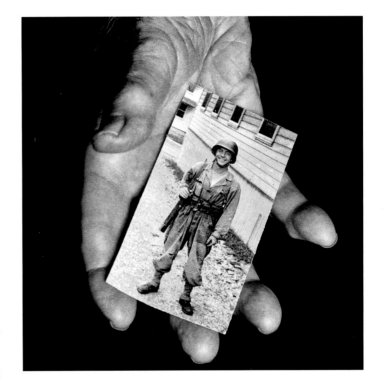

"My father used to read me the comics. He'd say, 'Morton, go down and get me the paper this morning.' I'd go get the paper, get in bed with him, [and] he would put his arm around me. He'd start reading *Moon Mullins* and tears of laughter would start streaming down his face. I'd think, 'Isn't that great to see your father laughing.' I decided then and there to be a cartoonist.

"I got drafted in 1942, and from the beginning I just fell into things. We were just getting ready to go overseas and I saw something about officer training school, so I signed up for that. Passed my test and was sent to training school and got a commission. They asked me what I wanted to do and I asked what do you recommend and they said if you volunteer to go overseas you get out sooner. I said I volunteer. The next thing I know I'm on a boat full of nurses. I met some sexy girls!

"We got to Naples and first thing they give me is being in charge of the POW camp with 10,000 Germans. I used to enjoy sitting down with them and talking. They had many questions about America. I was a good leader there. I wasn't mad or anything. I liked these guys. I didn't want to kill them. They were fascinated by our freedoms.

"I got away with murder in the army, so this is an inspiration for *Beetle Bailey*. I'm Beetle Bailey in a way."

Narissa Ferrer, 92
NAVY, WAVES
Seaman 2nd Class

Narissa had three brothers in the Army, so she joined the Navy. "I just wanted to be part of the whole thing and do my part." When asked if she had ever been on a ship, she said jokingly, "I never set foot on a ship. I was only on active duty for one year but maybe, if I had stayed in, I would have been on a ship and become an admiral."

Working as an illustrator on propaganda type materials for the military, Narissa worked on the fifth floor of a New York office building. There was no elevator and Narissa reports she lost thirty pounds in that year. Her memory of the propaganda she helped produce consists mainly of the theme of reminding the men on ships of the dangers of women on shore. They could be spies, agents, provocateurs, or manipulators. She says they were like comic books that played out scenes of what could happen to sailors on shore leave.

Narissa went on to become an actress on stage and screen, including several episodes of *The Phil Silvers Show* (Sgt. Bilko), and an artist.

Photo in hand: Narissa Ferrer is on right. Other veteran is unidentified.

Frank Borrelli, 91

ARMY

88th Division

ITALIAN CAMPAIGN

"I was an infantryman. I got wounded once. I was in (combat) two years until the war was over. I got hepatitis. I got polio once. I was in the hospital four times, each time for a month. That's what saved my life. The four times I came back from the hospital, I went back to nobody, I didn't know nobody.

"I climbed more mountains in Italy … you know what I did when I was climbing them mountains? I said to myself if I ever come out of this war I'm gonna drive from where we started in Naples all the way to the Alps. Thirty years later I did exactly that. I drove to every city my outfit fought in, right up to the Alps. I pissed on every mountain that I climbed. That was my vindication. I said, you son of a bitch, you, I told you I'd be back!

"One day we're being shelled by the Germans with mortars. You can hear them coming. Boy, I heard this one and I said, that son of a bitch, that one got my name on it. I'm done! I'm lying face down. Suddenly I heard Plunk! and I'm lookin' in the hole right in front of my face where the mortar landed. I'm waitin' for it to go off. I couldn't move anything, my nervous system was froze. I couldn't move a finger, I wanted to get up and run. I was so scared, I couldn't move nothing. And I'm lookin' in the hole, and after a few seconds, oh shit, must be a dud. I guess it saved my life. Phew, what a relief that was."

Edward Socha, 94

NAVY

USS *MARYLAND*

PEARL HARBOR

Ed remembers the first wave of Japanese torpedo planes came in at ten minutes to eight. The second wave, at ten.

"I was on the *Oklahoma* waiting for the motor launch to take me to church. I forgot my wallet so I went back [to the *Maryland*] to get it. When I got back the launch had gone. I'm standing there looking down the harbor and that's when the first one [Japanese warplane] flew right over me. He had dropped this torpedo. I thought it was one of our guys practicing. An ensign came running down the deck and said, 'Sound general quarters, those are Jap planes.' So I immediately went back to my ship next door. I ran up three decks to my battle station and looked over the side and the *Oklahoma* was flipped over. That quick, five minutes. Six torpedoes had hit the *Oklahoma* by the time I got up to my battle station on the *Maryland*. I had just been standing on the deck of the *Oklahoma* waiting to go to church.

"The whole harbor erupted. We were inboard [of the *Oklahoma*], I think that's what they did for the flagship of the admiral, for safety reasons. The oil on the water was burning. Coxswains in motor boats were going in there, picking up people. I was at my battle station and could hear tapping on the hull of the *Oklahoma*. They were cutting into the hull, they had the torches out already.

"You don't know what you were faced with. War was declared the next day. We geared up pretty damn quickly.

Oh man, how did they ever do it? The Marines came. The Seabees came out there. I mean doing what they did then, we'd probably all been in jail. It's just amazing, amazing."

Stanley J. Filimon, 94
ARMY
Specialist 4

ITALY • FRANCE • GERMANY

"We moved with the Army, about 3–5 miles behind the frontlines. We took care of the mortars. They were 4.2-inch mortars. We delivered them to the boys up front. The artillery pounded all night long for three years."

Stanley first landed at Naples, Italy, which had been secured, but the war was still raging up the road at Monte Casino. They unloaded the mortars and stored them in the caves under Naples which opened in the bay. The Germans had been using them for their U-boats.

"We had about 50,000 boxes of mortar shells. Two to a box. We secured them in the caves and began sending them to the front. We got word back that the mortars were landing short because of moisture in the powder rings. That's what determines how far a mortar went. Our CO had the brilliant idea of hanging them on a broom handle over a stove to dry them. They caught fire. The Naples Fire Department came and we were told to get the hell out of there. We were about fifty yards away and there was an explosion. Firetrucks came flying out of the cave and the captain of the department was killed along with several firemen. That happened on Christmas Eve. We were lucky to get out in time.

"I went overseas unassigned, you know, like raw meat. So, they go through your file to determine what your talents are. My expertise was, I got pulled from the Signal Corps as a switchboard operator. That's what saved me from being

picked for the infantry. Never saw a switchboard though. There weren't any.

"I landed in Naples and followed the Army for three years. First, north through Italy and then into France. Went north through Marseille to Mannheim, Germany. I was there when the war ended and I had just met up with my brother whose unit had just rolled in as the war ended. We were very happy to have made it."

Marvin Korff, 91
NAVY
Electronics Technician

USS *SAVANNAH*

"I enlisted in the navy out of high school. I was sent for college classes in engineering and electronics. I selected Oklahoma. Why? Because it was my first chance of getting away from home. And, they had the most beautiful girls on campus there.

"I was assigned to the USS *Savannah* after my schooling. Before I came aboard, the *Savannah* had been badly damaged at Salerno, Italy, and the captain had been told he could scuttle the ship. Instead, the ship went to Malta for three months of repairs and then to the Philadelphia Navy Yard for a year of repairs.

"After the repairs were completed we were assigned to go to the Pacific with the fleet headed for the invasion of Japan. The fleet started out in the afternoon and we watched them turn south one by one. We went to sleep waiting our turn to head south. I wake up and the engines are turning over. The ship is heading out. We get up in the morning and the sun is in our eyes. We wonder why are we heading due east? We go east for a few days. Then we meet up with a different task force. It includes the heavy cruiser USS *Quincy*. Then we find out, and I don't know exactly how we found out, maybe someone saw him, we were escorting President Roosevelt to the Yalta Conference to meet Churchill and Stalin. There was only about fifty yards between us and the *Quincy*. Our job was to get between any sound contact and the *Quincy* so we would take any torpedo headed for the *Quincy*. The reason we got the job was when the *Savannah* was rebuilt the year before, they added a secondary hull below the waterline to protect us from a torpedo penetrating to the ammunition magazine.

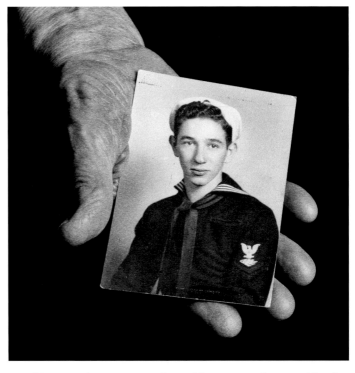

"During the trip across I would go up on the signal bridge and look at Roosevelt just about every day through binoculars. He looked like an old sick man.

"We dropped Roosevelt off at the island of Malta from where he went to the Yalta Conference with Churchill to meet Stalin. Before they went they had an open convertible motorcade through the streets of Malta, which I witnessed. That was thrilling to me."

John Parvin, 99
ARMY
Armored Artillery

EUROPE, 3rd ARMY ARMOR

"It was 1940. I was at the movies and saw an advertisement to join the military. So, I said to my girlfriend, I think I'll find out what it's all about. I went to the local armory and signed up. But I didn't know they were putting me on active duty the next day! Now I'm a private and they gave me a half-assed uniform." When John completed his military career, he left as a lieutenant colonel.

"By 1942, I went to officer training school to be a second lieutenant. I joined Gen. Patton's Army Armor School for Tanks. I became battalion motor officer for the 14th Armored Division and promoted to captain. That's in Patton's army. One day I was bringing up damaged vehicles to the front. I stopped because one of my tanks was in a ditch. Just then Patton comes rolling by. Patton yells, 'Who's in charge here?' I say, 'I am Sir.' He lets loose with language you couldn't describe. By that time, I had half my ass chewed out. 'Get those vehicles up to the front,' he says. Then he says, 'What's those sand bags on that tank?' I say, 'That's to deflect incoming fire.' He yells, '*Get those damn sand bags off the tanks. This is an offensive outfit, not defensive outfit!*'

"So, the next time I'm going down the road. I see one of my men with a broken-down tank. It needs a starter. Just then, here comes Patton up the road. He yells, 'Oh, it's you again! Did you get those sand bags off?' 'Yes sir,' I say. 'What are you doing here?' he yells. I say, 'Trying to repair this tank.' He chews the other half of my ass out.

'Get it out of my way,' says Patton. 'You're holding up the column.' I say to my warrant officer, 'Open the hatch and let me hear the engine. OK, take the eighth spark plug wire off and try again.' *Brummm*, it started right off. I lucked out on this one. The guys looked around and couldn't believe it worked."

John remembers being in Reims, France, site of the German surrender on May 7, 1945. "I was behind the school house when the German generals entered in the front. There was a big commotion. Afterwards, I got a copy of the surrender document which they passed out to the guys that were there." John finally says, "I can't remember anything else. All I was thinking about was getting home and getting a piece of ass."

Lt. Col. Parvin was awarded the Bronze Star for saving a tank crew from drowning after the tank ran off the road and sank.

"They're trying to kill me and I'm trying to kill them, that's the whole idea of the game."

Benjamin Ferencz, Army, Chief Prosecutor, Nuremberg War Trials

See page 93

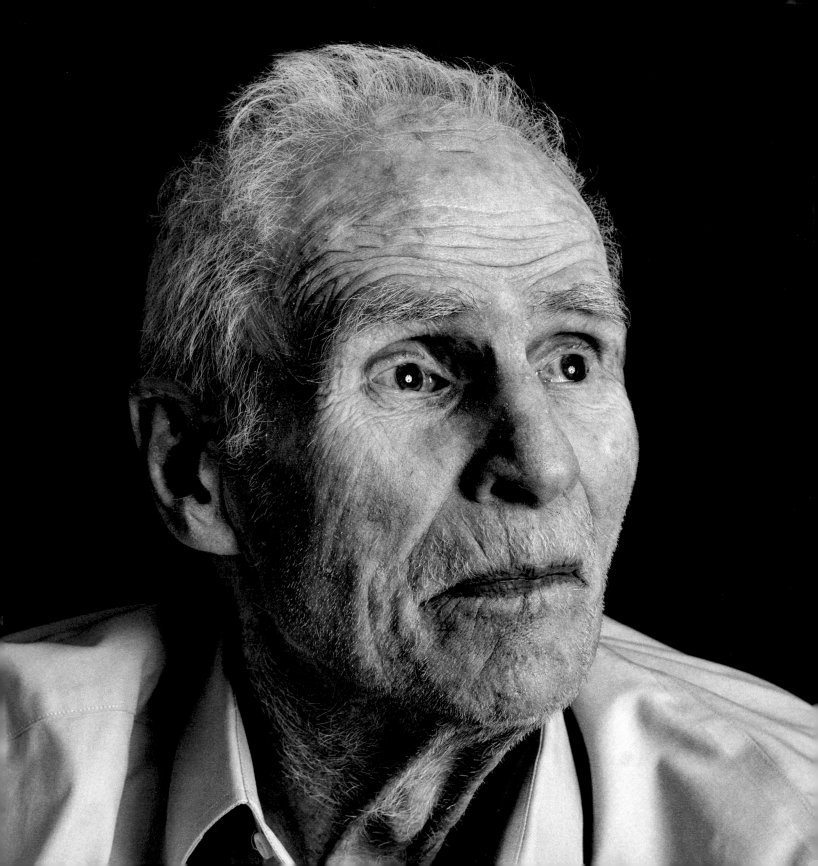

Brendan Byrne, 94
ARMY AIR FORCE
Governor of New Jersey

EUROPE, 50 MISSIONS
DISTINGUISHED FLYING CROSS

Governor Byrne enlisted in the Army Air Force in March 1943. As the youngest squadron navigator in his bomb group, he earned the Distinguished Flying Cross and four Air Medals. He attained the rank of lieutenant with the 414th Bomb Squadron of the 15th Air Force.

"We flew out of Foggia Air Base in Italy. The Tuskegee Airmen flew cover for us part way to Germany. They couldn't go the whole way. Not enough gas. It was scary.

"'Let's get the hell outta here!' That's what the crew always said after we dropped our last bomb.

"We got hit every time we flew. The B-17 was an amazing airplane. It could still fly full of holes and two engines gone."

Governor Byrne was a beloved two term governor of New Jersey. He is credited with saving what's known as the Pine Barrens.

The Pine Barrens territory helps recharge the 17 trillion gallon Kirkwood–Cohansey aquifer containing some of the purest water in the United States. Because of these factors, in 1978, Congress passed legislation to designate 1.1 million acres of the Pine Barrens as the Pinelands National Reserve (the nation's first National Reserve) to preserve its ecology.

New Jersey Governor Brendan Byrne: The Man Who Couldn't Be Bought, is a biography written by his former counsel, Donald Linky. Byrne is known for his sense of humor. While governor he quipped, "You know I look out this window at the Delaware River and I figured if I walked across the water, the headlines next day would say 'Byrne Can't Swim.'"

William DeGraf, 91
ARMY
West Point, First in Class, 1950

WORLD WAR II • KOREA • VIETNAM

"I enlisted in 1943, seventeen years old. The Army said we'll send you to college in the Army Specialized Reserve Program. I was at the University of Utah when my father called and said I'd gotten an appointment to West Point. So, they sent me to Cornell to start my training for West Point. But I failed the physical because of sinusitis. They said we need replacements in Europe so I joined the 100th division. They put me on the boat and we headed to southern France. We joined the 6th Army Group and were sent up the Rhone Valley into the Rouge Mountains. I was out front scouting when the shooting started. My buddy had just been killed about ten feet in front of me and I was lying flat on my stomach in snow. A bullet went under me and cut my bandolier off. That was my first day of combat. A couple of days later I got word I'd gotten another appointment to West Point. They sent me back to the rear to get a physical. Of course, I'd been up all night long, in combat, I hadn't had too much sleep, and the doctor said, 'Read that eye chart,' and I said what eye chart and he said go back to your company. There went my second appointment.

"We headed to a small French town, Rimling. My company commander put me in for a battlefield commission. They made me a second lieutenant, six days after my nineteenth birthday. According to the National Order of Battlefield Commissions, which no longer exists, I was the youngest battlefield commission in World War II.

"It was January 1945, and we were starting the attack into the Siegfried Line. In March I took a night patrol in. A young captain from the Signal Corps [communications] decided he wanted to go with us. He was senior to me so I said okay, you're in charge. He made so much noise we got a bunch of hand grenades thrown at us and that ended my war. I was wounded and sent back to a hospital in France. By the time I got sent back to my company, the war was over.

"Just about that time, I got my third appointment to West Point. I wore glasses all through World War II. I had 20/70 vision. I knew I couldn't read the eye chart. I found a doctor who prescribed eye exercises and I passed the physical this time. I graduated June 6, 1950, got married June 10, and the war in Korea started June 23. I was off to my second war.

"After Korea, I stayed in the Army doing mostly teaching, including at West Point. In 1969, I got a friend of mine at the Pentagon to send me to Vietnam as a brigade commander. I was a colonel by this point. I commanded the 1st Brigade of the 1st Division (The "Big Red One") in Vietnam. That's three appointments to West Point and three wars."

What Col. DeGraf didn't mention in our interview was that he graduated first in his class at West Point in 1950. That is a very big deal.

"*I went from college right to the Army. I trained first to be an officer because all the boys in my class were going in to train as officers in the Navy. By golly, I was going to be an officer or I wasn't going in.*"

Joyce Robinson, Army WAC

See page 109

Frank Alexander Gregg, 94

ARMY

101st Airborne

JUMPED INTO NORMANDY ON D-DAY

"I was a first lieutenant and executive officer of a company in the 501st Regiment of the 101st Airborne Division. We jumped into Normandy, France the night before D-Day. As soon as we hit the coast of Normandy we started picking up machine gun fire. I would've sworn every German in Normandy had a machine gun firing at us. You could see the stream of tracers coming up and the pilot was taking evasive action not to fly through the streams. It was a very rough trip going into Normandy. Finally, the pilot hit the green to jump. We assumed the pilot knew where we were. We had a giant bundle of ammunition, mortars, and such that we were to push out and we would jump right after. When we started to push it out, the plane was rocking hard. We shoved it out and the thing got stuck in the door. So we said 'Oh goodness, we've got to get this thing loose and out the door!'

"It seemed like thirty minutes but of course it was less than five minutes. We got the bundle out and then we went out. Which means we were not over the place we were supposed to be, so we were scattered badly. There was nothing I could do to get out of the way of the stream of tracers. I knew every fifth bullet was a tracer. That means between every two tracers, there was four bullets I couldn't see.

"I saw we were going to land in water. I hit the water and it was knee-to-hip deep. I started looking around for my men. Nobody. Just nobody. And you talk about feeling alone, I felt alone. I was completely lost and so was all the other troops.

"Of course, it was still dark. I got up and started walking. I ran into some docile milk cows and I knew they must belong to someone. I started picking up paratroopers along the way and now there was about ten

89

of us. We found the farm the cows came from. I rapped on the door with my rifle, then a girl opened the door. I pointed to the US patch on my shoulder. She had no doubt I was the American force. I took a dripping wet map out of my pocket. We needed to find where we were. I spread the map out on a table. I said 'Bosch,' it was a word for German we both shared. She then pointed to a nearby church and said, 'Bosch.' I took my men down to that church but there were no Germans in there.

"So, we started up the road to the village and coming down the other way was my battalion commander. I told him I had now nineteen men, all from different units. He told me he was glad to see me. He then told me a large group of Germans were up the road. He told me to flank them and he was in front of them. Then I heard, 'Tank!' I thought 'Oh no. Just what I need.' But it was our tank oh boy, they can help us get to the place we needed to be. This was a tank that had just landed at D-Day. I asked him how [he] got here and he said, 'I don't know.' I got on the tank behind the turret with my men following. I told him which way to go and we ran into the Germans. We followed him like another coat of paint. He shot a tank round into road junction and the Germans started running out. He shot another tank round dead on target. The Germans all fell back. We moved up and captured the position. And that's essentially the end of the first day of D-Day, June 6, 1944. That's where I stopped the first day. We used their foxholes and made sure they couldn't come back."

"I was twenty-one years old and risk was what we did."

Michael Taras, Army Air Force, Pilot

See page 107

Benjamin Ferencz, 98
ARMY

EUROPE, 5 BATTLE STARS
CHIEF PROSECUTOR, NUREMBERG

Ben Ferencz is the last surviving chief prosecutor from the Nuremberg Trials. There were twelve separate trials that comprised the prosecution of Nazi war criminals. Mr. Ferencz's trial involved the *Einsatzgruppen* (SS/SD mobile killing units) who were responsible for the murder of over one million Jews and other people not tolerated by the Nazis. They were shot in cold blood in their homes or towns and not in concentration camps.

Mr. Ferencz joined the army after graduating from Harvard Law School. He spent his army career having to bear that burden. He was routinely given the worst jobs. He was told, "You clean the toilets." He said, "I did it and then was told, 'You can do better than that, you're a Harvard graduate. Do it again.'" He said, "I enlisted in the army because I didn't want anybody else dying for me!"

"I did spend time in the trenches. I was very fortunate. I guess the bullets went over my head [Mr. Ferencz is five feet tall.] They're trying to kill me and I'm trying to kill them, that's the whole idea of the game. Of course, the worse part was going into the concentration camps. Seeing how human beings could behave to other human beings. I got to know the mass murderers and their mentality. I lecture around the world and write books [about peace]. Eisenhower said, 'We have to eliminate war making. We can no longer rely on force to settle disputes. It's too dangerous. You must rely on the rule of law.' That's been my motto: 'Law Not War.'

"I was notorious. Before I was hired [as a Nuremberg Prosecutor] by my general, Telford Taylor, he said, 'I hear you're occasionally insubordinate.' I say, 'That's not correct sir, I'm not occasionally insubordinate, I'm usually insubordinate. I don't obey any order I know is illegal or stupid.' Taylor smiled and said, 'You come with me.' We became good friends and law partners after the war.

"Did I mention the Germans have given me their medal of honor, first-class? Very nice thing. If you want to film it, I'll give you a film with that around my neck. I look like Rommel. [Ben laughs.] I got it from the Germans—that's important. When I found out they wanted me to accept this medal, some of my friends, Holocaust survivors, say to me, 'Ben you shouldn't accept that from them.' I said, 'I'm going to think about it.' I thought about it. I decided I was going to accept it. Why? Because they were trying to say they were sorry. Remember it's the next generation—not the one that did it. It's the only way they could say sorry."

Benjamin Ferencz tells many unique and fascinating stories. He is an amazing man. His website benferencz. org is not to be missed. Read some of his stories under the tab "benny stories."

"Nothing else is on my conscience that I know about, except why I'm the only one of my friends that made it back."

Ben Skardon, Army, Bataan Death March Survivor

See page 97

Ben Skardon, 100
ARMY

THE PHILIPPINES
BATAAN DEATH MARCH

The US Army had sent advisors to the Philippines prior to the outbreak of war to help the Philippine Army prepare for a Japanese invasion. Ben Skardon was a newly-minted captain, arriving just in time for that invasion. After about four months of fierce fighting the Japanese seized the island. It was 1942. Skardon says, "The Japanese told us we were captives, not prisoners of war, and [that] they'd treat us any way they wanted to. So, we were treated like animals—worse than animals." Filipino and American prisoners of war, 60,000–80,000 of them, were forced to march by the Imperial Japanese Army for eighty miles to a prison camp. The march was characterized by severe abuse and murder. It was later judged by the Allies military commission to be a Japanese war crime.

After the march. the Japanese attempted to move the prisoners by boat to Japan several times. Some were sunk by US bombs. These boats were to become known as "The Hell Ships." Ben was on one of the worst: the *Ōryoku Maru*. He recalls:

"They were loading about 1,600 of us into the holds of a ship. We were so crammed in we were suffocating. We then were attacked by our own planes and we wished the bombs would hit us so we could escape. That segment of our trip was one of the most horrible of all things. I knew about the Black Hole of Calcutta. I thought this was worse. At this time, you can't give up." Incredibly,

Skardon survived the sinking of two other unmarked Japanese transport ships carrying him and other POWs to mainland Japan.

Skardon eventually ended up in a prison camp in Manchuria, where Russian units freed him in August

1945. He was twenty-seven years old and weighed ninety pounds.

"My son married a half Japanese girl. When they were here once I asked her to retype some of my speeches for me [about the war]. I noticed when I got the copies back that 'Japs' had been replaced with 'Japanese.' I said to my son John, 'I see that 'Japs' have been changed to 'Japanese.'' 'Dad,' he said, 'You insulted her.' I said, 'How was that?' [My son said] 'When you are giving your speeches, you're saying Japs. That's the same as a four-letter word.' Well, that kind of crushed me. So, I apologized to Niko. I told her I had no idea that existed. She was hurt badly. I tell you that because I've been up and down the ladder so much. We are talking about soldiers, not the Japanese people. I'm making that clear because it's on my conscience. Nothing else is on my conscience that I know about, except why I'm the only one of my friends that made it back."

"When Churchill made his speech the day after the surrender, I was in that crowd. I remember seeing he was drunk as a Cooter. He was a big drinker as people know."

Edward T. Ziegler, Army

See page 117

George Schaller, 93
NAVY
USS *PENSACOLA*

IWO JIMA

"Me and my buddy didn't want to be drafted so we went down and signed up with the Navy. My buddy got tuberculosis and spent four years in a TB hospital. And I spent three years in the Navy.

"I became a yeoman on the USS *Pensacola*. We had seven engagements with the Japanese before getting to Iwo Jima. When I saw Iwo Jima for the first time, it was just rock and black sand. I was wounded during the bombardment of Iwo. My duty station on the *Pensacola* was on the secondary bridge. I was a phone talker. The barrage of shells from the island hit our funnel [the ship's smokestack] and shrapnel was going everywhere. That's how I got hit. I remember looking up and the funnel looked like a sieve! That was it for me. I spent fourteen months in the hospital.

"I was evacuated by a Higgins boat [that was] to take us to the hospital ship. It got dark so the hospital ship left and we were just left bobbing in the ocean in this bathtub! [A Higgins boat is open to the elements.] The hospital ship came back the next day and took us to Saipan.

"The heavy cruiser USS *Pensacola* was sent to Bikini Island after the war to be a target for the atomic bomb tests. It survived and was ultimately sunk off Washington, DC while being used as a target ship."

H.J. Lark, 95
ARMY AIR FORCE
Pilot B-24 Liberator

NINE MISSIONS TO PLOIEȘTI OILFIELDS

Lt. H.J. Lark commanded a B-24 Liberator with a crew of ten. He was twenty-two years old. He was credited with fifty missions. Lt. Lark was given only initials on his birth certificate. He was told by his parents that when he came of age, he should choose his own name. He never did. When he joined the army, they were adamant that he needed a name. He stood firm. The army put his name on the official enlistment document as "H.(only) J.(only) Lark." Of course, he got the nickname Holy Joly!

H.J. doesn't say much anymore. His son gave me a magazine article H.J. wrote a few years back about a terrifying mission. He called it Black Ploiești. Ploiești is the oil rich area in Romania which the Germans counted on for their fuel. Understanding that the fuel was key, the Germans made this site one of the most heavily fortified in Europe.

I've paraphrased from that article here:

On July 9, 1944, Lark and his crew were muttering epithets of frustration about having to go over Ploiești one more time. This was the crew's fourth time. When we arrived on target a single shell exploded high above the formation. It made a red smoke hang in the sky. Seconds later the sky erupted with a mélange of flak. As they reached the bomb run and made the turn, Lark said that the flak was surely the worst that they had ever experienced. Exploding anti-aircraft shells have three

distinct sounds: *brrumph*, *crraack*, and *powwow*. *Brrumph* is close enough to hear but far enough away to ignore; *crraack* causes one to flinch or to duck. The explosive *pow-wow* signals a hit. Just after turning onto the bomb run, they get hit. Suddenly, Lark hears, "Engineer to pilot, we've got a fire." Their plane's load that day was incendiary bombs—making any kind of fire on the plane more dangerous than anything else. Saving the crew became Lark's major concern. Lark makes his decision and says, "Drop 'em." They soon discovered the fire had been caused by flak that had come through the flight deck and passed through cotton padding of the bench seat; the shrapnel was hot enough to ignite the cotton. They hoped they could turn for home now, but it wasn't over. Twelve Me 109s [German fighter aircraft] jumped their bomb squadron and everyone opened fire. After a brief flurry of fire, the German fighters broke off the attack. The squadron finally closed ranks and headed for home. Lark comments, "We closed it up tightly and ran for home. Never before had I flown so close to another airplane."

"I've been going down to the World War II Memorial in Washington every Saturday for six years to greet all the veterans … You know we can sit there and tell each other lies because we know there's nobody old enough to contradict us. So, we're all heroes."

Bob Dole, Army, US Senator

See page 113

Michael Taras, 94
ARMY AIR FORCE
C-47 Transport Pilot

"I wanted to be a twin-engine pilot in the war. I went into the Army Air Force in 1942 hoping to become a P-38 pursuit fighter pilot. Instead they sent me for the C-47 training [transport aircraft] program.

"We went to Brighton, England. Our mission was to supply Gen. Patton's tank corps with gasoline. We followed his army across France flying in full loads of five gallon cans with 90-octane gas. We landed just behind the front lines, unloaded, and got out of there as fast as we could. We would do this day after day. There was no fifty mission limit like bomber pilots had. It was risky. I knew one bullet could blow up the whole plane. I was twenty-one years old and risk was what we did.

"When the war was over we stayed on as an airline for generals and bigwigs. One nice mission my crew and I got was to fly a group of war correspondents around to all the airfields in the Mediterranean and Middle East. I picked these guys up in Wiesbaden, Germany, then on to Marseille. From there it was Rome, Athens, Cairo, Bagdad, Istanbul, and back. A fellow couldn't ask for a better closure to his time in Europe. I can remember once taking off out of Bagdad—this is all before GPS and air traffic control—and there's a huge storm over the mountains. I had to get down and around without hitting the mountains and find my way home. I guess I did it. I'm here! The junket was both the best and the worst.

"Now, when I think about flying around with a plane full of gasoline, it was scary."

The military C-47 aircraft is the same airplane as the commercial DC-3 which has been in service around the world to this day.

Joyce Robinson, 96
ARMY

US PENTAGON • JAPAN

Joyce spent the war years in the basement of the Pentagon decoding messages and writing daily reports for the general officers. After the war, she went to Japan with the Army of Occupation. Here is her story:

"I went from college right to the Army. I trained first to be an officer because all the boys in my class were going in to train as officers in the Navy. By golly, I was going to be an officer or I wasn't going in.

"They decided since I had a bachelor's degree in English that I should do something about writing. So, they sent me up to Washington to the Pentagon. I was in charge of writing the daily news reports for the admirals and generals. I'd get all the messages in, decode them, and write reports for the officers. I did all the South America messages. We were in the basement of the Pentagon. It was a secret place. We were locked in a room with guards inside and outside. They had guns.

"After a year and half at the Pentagon, they decided I was going to learn Japanese. I wasn't even asked. 'You have Spanish, English, French, and German,' they said. They sent me for a year to the University of Michigan for Japanese. So, when the war was over they said, 'You know Japanese, you're going to Japan.' During the war women couldn't have guns. Now I had to take a shooting course. But my boyfriend pretended to be helping me and he shot the [target] because I couldn't."

In Japan, Capt. Robinson supervised a group of highly educated Japanese men whose job was to translate internal communications into English. It was a form of keeping tabs on what the Japanese were saying amongst themselves.

"I still couldn't read Japanese. There was a young American man who was assigned to me who was bilingual. He lived in Japan with his missionary parents. I had him check the translation of the many men working for me. Every once in a while, he found something they forgot to tell me, you know, like something vital. Once, I called a man who had left something out up in front of me, and said, 'Did you translate this?' And he said, 'Yes ma'am.' I said, 'You're fired.' And I didn't have to fire anybody after that.

"We worked in an enormous post office building in Tokyo. It had radiators around this huge room. The head [Japanese] guy asked me, 'Could they put their lunches on the radiators?' I said, 'Oh, yes.' The stink of fish! All my American friends were furious with me. I told them I couldn't tell them no now. The Japanese people were docile, docile, docile, because the Emperor and Gen. McArthur told them to do whatever we said."

. . . *"The door drops down and the two guys on either side of me get picked off, they never step off the boat."*

Arthur Gendler, Army, D-Day

See page 65

Bob Dole, 94
ARMY
10th Mountain Division

ITALY

US SENATOR

Senator Dole enlisted in the Army in 1942. He went to Ft. Benning for officer training and was commissioned a second lieutenant. He joined the Army's 10th Mountain Division and was sent to Italy as a replacement officer. As Dole recalls in his book *One Soldier's Story*, his type of officer was known among the men as a "90-day wonder." After being sent to the front to replace a fallen second lieutenant and to command a platoon, Dole said the men avoided getting to know him, fearing that he too would get killed soon. In April of 1945, while leading a charge against a German machine gun nest, Dole was badly wounded. Dole had sustained the following injuries: a shattered right shoulder, fractured vertebrae in his neck and spine, paralysis from the neck down, metal shrapnel throughout his body and a damaged kidney. Medics did not expect him to recover. He defied all odds. He survived and endured a grueling four-year recovery process. Some of his wounds linger today. He has become a great advocate for all veterans.

"I returned to Ft. Benning recently to attend a graduation ceremony. The class of second lieutenants were very impressive. There were many women, many of them African-American, which really made me feel good. You know the women and men go through the exact same training. I left there with a high feeling. I think our country is going to be in good shape with young people like this.

"I've been going down to the World War II Memorial in Washington every Saturday for six years to greet all the veterans. I have met so many wonderful veterans. You know we can sit there and tell each other lies because we know there's nobody old enough to contradict us. So, we're all heroes. We have a lot of fun there.

"I came to Congress in 1961. I served under President Eisenhower for about three months. He's a fellow Kansan and a personal hero of mine. After seventy-two years, finally, we're going to build an Eisenhower memorial here in the Capitol. I volunteer with the people who are making this happen. I've been trying to raise money for the project. I call some of these young CEOs for some money. They know a little about World War II, but they don't know Eisenhower, especially like someone [like me] who knew him. They tell me their charity budget isn't big enough to give me much money. I say it's not charity I'm asking for, it's payment! Recognition for this man who literally saved this country, is long overdue."

"I never set foot on a ship … if I had stayed in [the Navy], I would have been on a ship and become an admiral."

Narissa Ferrer, Navy Waves

See page 69

Edward T. Zeigler, 93
ARMY
Office Manager

ENGLAND

"My friends call me Ziggy. I was in the signal corps of the transportation corps. I got to England before D-Day. We took orders for transportation equipment and made sure everybody got what they ordered. I was in charge of the office, really. The major just said to me, 'Be good and don't mess up.' My major and sergeant used to go out together and get drunk and did bad things. I don't drink or smoke or own a boat. I covered up for them.

"We started doing dry runs for D-Day preparation. Everyone knew it was coming, even the Germans. One day the major comes in and says, 'Today's the day. It's not a dry run.' The invasion of Europe was on. We watched the planes leave; they filled the sky. When they came back there were not as many. You could hear some of them putt-putting, trying to make the airfield.

"When Churchill made his speech the day after the surrender, I was in that crowd. I remember seeing he was drunk as a Cooter. He was a big drinker as people know. We just happened to be there. We were lucky. I remember, I was climbing up a light post so I could see more. As I came down this girl started to kiss me and she didn't have a tooth in her head. I pulled my head away quick. We were doing dances in the street. We were just as happy as those English people. Churchill came out on a balcony. There were a million people there. I think it was Trafalgar Square."

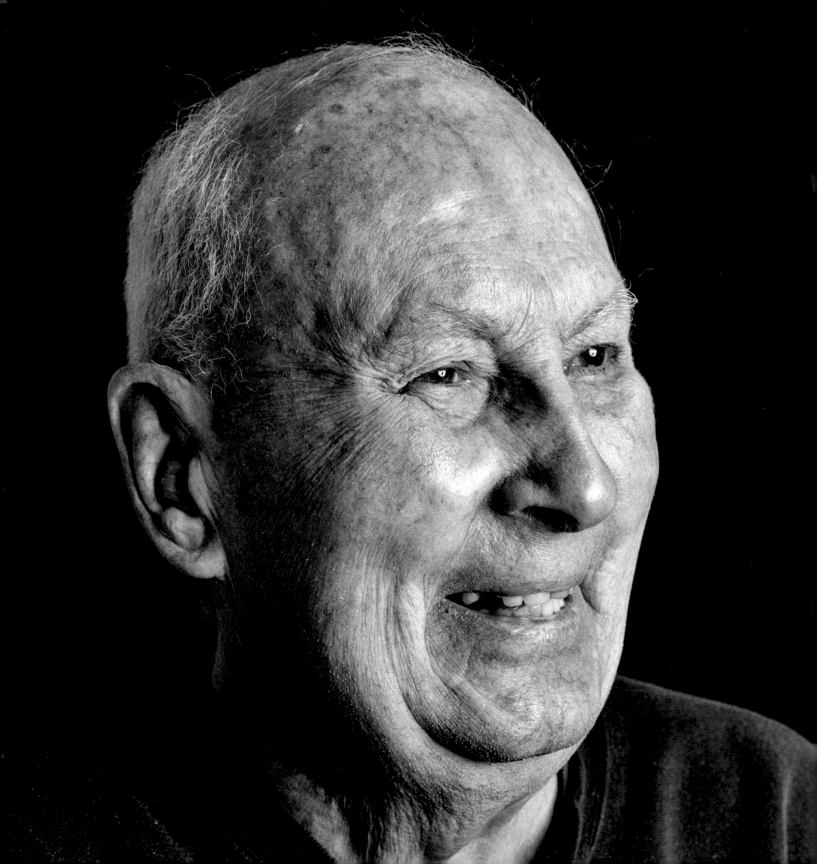

Russell Collins, 91
NAVY

BATTLESHIP USS *NEW JERSEY*

"My parents had to sign for me. I was seventeen years old when I joined the Navy in 1943. After all my training I was assigned to the USS *New Jersey*. We went to the South Pacific and did a lot of island bombardment. We worked together with the USS *Iowa*. I remember bombarding Iwo Jima and Tinian.

"We were in the Battle of the Philippine Sea. We had over 400 Jap planes coming at us. They called that part of the battle the 'Marianas Turkey Shoot.' We shot down five kamikaze planes. We went topside because we weren't going to be shooting 16-inch shells at airplanes. We were standing on the main deck and watching at least two dozen dogfights. We're firing at these airplanes and we don't know who's chasing who. They finally came over the loud speaker and said cease firing. Were in the biggest battle of the war and they're telling cease fire. Well, we were shooting at our own planes.

"Halsey's Typhoon, we were in that. The ship took a 37-degree list. We lost three destroyers. They capsized. We were caught in the typhoon for three days. We were in one-hundred foot waves. I was on watch next to a search light. I saw the bow and the number one turret go completely underwater.

"After the typhoon, we went to Ulithi for rest and repairs. We looked out from our ship and saw guys on a passing tugboat putting on lifejackets. And then we saw splashes in the water. Then a shell came and went

through our back deck, into the mess hall, through the third deck and rested in the bottom of the ship. It was a dud, it didn't explode. It was a shell from target practice that was taking place outside the harbor by our own guys. They got too close. It was the only time the *New Jersey* got hit by a shell.

"I was standing in the canteen line. I was probably going to get cigarettes. There were two sailors ahead of me. We're standing there and the orderly comes through and says, 'Attention!' Adm. 'Bull' Halsey comes in and says, 'At ease,' and gets in line right behind me. This is an admiral, he could start his own line whenever he wants. But we all understand he was for the enlisted man. One or two minutes later a young ensign comes through the hatch and sees a line standing there, so he's gonna start his own line. So, he started on the other side and Halsey steps out and says 'Sir, the end of the line starts here.' And this ensign says, 'Yes sir.' He got as red as a thermometer. He went around and stands right behind Adm. Halsey. True story!"

"They had swastikas hung up like Yankee championship banners. We shelled it until it was dust."

Herbert Stevens, Army Artillery

See page 35

Charles Cleaver, 99

NAVY

Supply Corps

USS ATASCOSA

Mr. Cleaver enlisted in the Navy right after graduating from Harvard Business College. That was 1942. After training and some stateside duty, he was assigned to sea aboard the USS *Atascosa*, a supply ship. Here are some excerpts from his memoir.

"The USS *Atascosa* was a fleet oiler, designed for refueling at sea. On one trip, our sister ship USS *Cache* met us returning with a hole in her side from a Jap torpedo—a reminder that we were really at war. In early 1944, with Guadalcanal secure, and as more troop and ships became available, islands like Guam, Saipan, Iwo Jima were invaded. We became involved in our primary mission—refueling the fleet, usually while the attacks were ongoing, or soon after the islands were taken.

"In early December 1944, while providing secondary support to MacArthur's invasion of the Philippines, Typhoon Cobra hit—a severe blow to the Navy comparable to the Coral Sea defeat and Midway. While cruising about 300 miles east of the Philippines, Halsey took the fleet into the eye of the storm. Waves were so high that ships low on fuel rolled sixty or more degrees. Three capsized. Our ship was damaged. I was hit on the head by a heavy light while helping clear a cargo boom. Took three stitches. Only my steel helmet prevented a concussion.

"Operating from Ulithi, we were again busy fueling at sea. In early 1945, the big push by the Fifth Fleet to the Philippines, Okinawa, and Japan started. At one point, there were Navy ships spread out in every direction as far as I could see and they all needed supplies, especially fuel. It was like a gigantic service station with the supply ships spread out to the horizon. When a large ship would move up on our port beam, hoses would be connected, held up with large steel booms, and we would transfer oil and aviation gas for an hour or more. At the same time, smaller ships like destroyers would come alongside on the starboard, fuel hoses would be connected and after perhaps half an hour, another would take its place.

"In May 1945, I was ordered to the large supply depot at Mare Island, Vallejo, California, twenty miles north of San Francisco, as receiving officer. More really dull duty. I remained there until January 1946, when I was separated from the Navy, returned home, and started looking for a job."

"I lecture around the world and write books [about peace]. Eisenhower said, 'We have to eliminate war making. We can no longer rely on force to settle disputes. It's too dangerous. You must rely on the rule of law.' That's been my motto: 'Law Not War.'"

Benjamin Ferencz, Army, Chief Prosecutor, Nuremberg War Trials

See page 93

RICHARD BELL

A lifelong photojournalist and commercial photographer, Richard Bell started his career as a biology major at Kent State University. After witnessing the shootings at Kent, Richard switched his major to journalism. Jobs at two large metropolitan daily papers followed: *The St. Petersburg Times* and *The Philadelphia Inquirer*. At the *Inquirer*, Richard moved from staff photojournalist to photo editor where he was awarded the Newspaper Photo Editor of the Year award from the Pictures of the Year competition (POY). Leaving the newspaper business Richard started his own commercial photography business, The Bing Group, which produced print advertising for business uses. Concurrently he was a senior lecturer at the University of the Arts in Philadelphia, teaching documentary photography. Richard is currently working on fine art, book projects, and documentary projects from his office.